Rescue Chopper

A HIWAY BOOK

Westminster HIWAY Books by
Ruth Hallman

Rescue Chopper

Midnight Wheels

Gimme Something, Mister!

I Gotta Be Free

Secrets of a Silent Stranger

Rescue Chopper

Ruth Hallman

HIWAY

𝓦

The Westminster Press
Philadelphia

First edition

PUBLISHED BY THE WESTMINSTER PRESS®
PHILADELPHIA, PENNSYLVANIA

PRINTED IN THE UNITED STATES OF AMERICA

9 8 7 6 5 4 3 2 1

Library of Congress Cataloging in Publication Data

Hallman, Ruth, 1929–
  Rescue chopper.

  "A Hiway book."
  SUMMARY: Eleven episodes featuring a Coast
Guard search and rescue team which, despite a certain
amount of internal rivalry, manages to effect some
dangerous helicopter rescues.
  [1. Rescue work—Fiction]   I. Title
PZ7.H15469Re   [Fic]   80–15593
ISBN 0–664–32667–6

To Lieutenant Commander Dave Jeffrey, USCG,
for so generously and patiently giving
his expert technical advice

Special Acknowledgment for Assistance:

Lt. Comdr. Richard Cottingham, USCG

Comdr. W. H. Hall, USCG

Capt. Ara E. Midgett, Commanding Officer,
USCG Air Station, Elizabeth City, N.C.

Nicholas J. Ali, Lt. Comdr., USNR

Gates S. Murchie, Lt., USNR

Robert E. Hallman

Contents

1
Call
for Help

The shrill noise of the siren rose over the riverbanks. Men stopped to hear the voice of the duty officer. His words came loud and clear.

"Fishing boat thirty miles off Cape Lookout. Man with head wound."

In the mess hall, pilot Scott Keane shoved his chair away from the table. His heavy black boots thudded across the floor. Steam still rose from the hot food left on his tray. He raced out of the Coast Guard building.

Scott ran out on the road to the hangars. His orange flight suit was bright against the dark road. In his mind he checked the things to be done before lifting off in the HH3F.

"Sir," a voice gasped behind him. A short man in the same kind of orange suit trailed Scott. "Sir—Commander Keane, are you going to beat your own time getting off to this rescue? Sounds like it's about the same spot off the Cape as that call we had Friday."

Scott turned. His radioman, Vince, was chugging right along in step with him. Scott grinned at the younger man. For two years they had flown together as part of a search and rescue crew.

"You keep pushing me to do better, Vince. What's the matter? Do you have a bet on with another helicopter crew? Do you want to be sure we are the fastest?" Scott ran along easily on strong legs.

Vince grinned. He was puffing for breath now. The hangar was only three hundred yards from the mess hall, but Vince had just finished a big meal. He looked as if his stomach ached with each jar of his pounding legs.

Pilot and crewman ran across the blacktop. They looked over at the helicopter standing on the ready line. Men in the ground crew were quickly adding fuel to the aircraft.

A low-slung blue car tore into the parking lot next to the hangar. A man in white tennis shorts climbed out of the driver's bucket seat. Hopping along on one foot, he yanked on an orange flight suit. The long zipper stuck.

"Wait, Scott!" the man called to the pilot. The man did not even nod to Vince. He called again to Scott, "Wait, I say!"

Scott stopped by the office door of the hangar. He watched the heavyset co-pilot fight with the zipper of the suit. Wade was a fine flier. More than once Scott had been grateful for Wade's skills with the HH3F. But the co-pilot did not know how to work with other people. The radioman, the flight mechanic, and the ground crew meant nothing to Wade. They were there only to be used for his needs. Scott felt this did not help the crew work well together.

This bright Monday in September would be no bet-

ter. Wade would be at his worst, because a new flight mechanic was joining the crew. A new crewman was the bottom line in the co-pilot's eyes.

"I just heard the tag end of the alarm—man hurt. I had a good tennis game going with Harris. Didn't catch everything the duty officer said. Where are we going?" Wade asked.

The co-pilot always talked about his tennis games. He claimed he skipped lunch when he used the tennis courts near the hangar. Scott laughed to himself. He knew Wade stuffed his mouth in the car ride from the courts to the hangar.

"It's the Cape again, Wade. Let's check with the duty officer. I want to see where that boat is. We got a forecast of good weather this morning. At least that part is okay!"

The two pilots ran into the offices. They looked through the glass wall of the map room. A Coast Guard officer was bending over a huge table. The map on the table showed the Fifth District area of the United States Coast Guard. The group of buildings at Elizabeth City, North Carolina, was the center of Coast Guard aviation. It had an air station, an air base, and a repair and supply center. Scott, Wade, and the duty officer bent over the map. The duty officer pointed to the site of the call for help.

"It won't take you long, Scott." The duty officer looked at the pilot. "But don't waste any time. The call came in from another fishing party boat. Said this boat's captain was pretty worried. Had a man bleeding heavily from a head wound. Lots of blood lost already. I don't know any more facts."

There was a crash from the outside office. A chair fell

against the door. All three officers looked up quickly. Another orange-suited figure slowly picked up the chair. The young man set the chair back in place with a thump. Wade frowned at the sound.

"What is it? Don't tell me it's something I'm going to have to put up with," he said loudly.

Scott strode out of the map room. The pilot put out his hand. He firmly shook the hand of the new crewman.

"Glad to see you again, Cal! Welcome to the crew. We are ready for takeoff as soon as we check our flight plan. We'll be right out." He clapped a hand on the young man's back.

Cal grinned just a little. He brushed at the clumps of hair sticking up like pieces of straw. He pulled the orange sleeves down over his bony wrists. Then he turned and fell over the same chair. He picked up the chair again and made it safely out of the door.

The co-pilot was staring after the young man. "Scott, don't tell me that is our new flight mechanic! If he is, I think I'm ready to quit. He can't even take care of his own body—much less safely hoist someone who is hurt up to the helicopter!"

Scott leveled steady brown eyes at the co-pilot. "That is our new flight mechanic. His name is Cal Grimes. He has a fine record. And we are lucky he is to be a part of our crew. Now, let's get a move on!"

Scott turned quickly. After one more glance at the map, he went out the door. He pulled the white Coast Guard helmet over his short brown hair. He snapped the strap as he ran.

Wade followed along. He stopped only once to tie his left black boot. They ran through the big empty hangar.

The bright sunshine blinded them after the darkness of the cave-like building.

The radioman and the flight mechanic were already in their seats. The radioman hunched over the little "black box." It held the machine that told how to steer their course. The radioman sat on the left, behind the co-pilot.

Scott settled into the pilot's seat on the right. "Everything check out okay, Cal?" he asked the new crewman.

"Set and ready to go, sir," the flight mechanic said. Wade looked up in surprise at the change in Cal's voice. He did not sound like the same clumsy crewman who had fallen over the chair in the office. There was a strong sureness in his voice. Wade shook his head.

The co-pilot climbed past the new man. He strapped himself into his own seat next to the pilot. Cal closed the door of the chopper. He fastened his own seat straps. His movements were quick and sure.

The checklists were soon finished. The aircraft was cleared to takeoff. The helicopter lifted off in a chattering arc across the river.

The Coast Guard buildings spread out under them. A winding road started at the guard station by the highway. It circled past work buildings, past the huge hangar. It wound around the quarters and mess halls for officers and enlisted men. The strip of road ran alongside the runways.

HH3F 1027 settled into its flight for Cape Lookout. A big C130 transport plane roared in past them for a landing. The huge plane was bringing in helicopter rotors to be worked on at the repair center.

Scott did not even glance at the C130. His thoughts

were already racing toward the rescue ahead of him and his crew. In his mind he checked each step to be taken. He had carried out many, many rescues. But each time was different. Each time, another person was in need of special help.

2
Floating Face Down

Scott had waited a long time to be pilot of a rescue helicopter. His training had been in the Navy. Then he joined the Coast Guard rescue service. When he signed up, three hundred pilots were seeking the job. Ten were chosen. He was number ten.

"HH3F 1027 reporting," Vince spoke over the radio. Every fifteen minutes he called in to home base. Every thirty minutes he would tell where they were.

"Start trying to reach the fishing boat on the radio, Vince," Scott said to the radioman.

Then he called over his shoulder to the new flight mechanic. "Did you check out the hoist? And what about the litter? Will you need anything else for rescue, Cal?"

"Everything is ready, sir. New floats should be placed on the litter before the next trip. It's okay for now."

"Right," said the pilot. "Be sure you speak loud and clear for the hoist. I want to hear how far I should go —which way to move. I don't like to keep turning my head to try and see. Hurts the neck after a while, okay?"

"Yes, sir," was the steady answer from the flight mechanic.

The co-pilot was busy with the chart between the two pilots' seats. This chart helped them steer their course.

"We should be able to talk by radio with the fishing boat anytime now. We are closing in on their site," the co-pilot reported to the pilot.

"Got them yet, Vince?" the pilot asked.

"Not yet, sir," the radioman said.

Scott looked down at the water below. The helicopter was whirling its way across Albemarle Sound. The pencil-thin islands of the Outer Banks stretched out under them. The chopper swept out over the ocean.

Very few whitecaps showed on the waves beneath them. The report for good weather was holding true. This rescue should be easy.

"Commander Keane, I have the fishing boat on the radio," Vince said into the mike in his helmet.

"Good! Ask them to say exactly where they are. Then report that to the Portsmouth Rescue Center."

"Yes, sir," came the reply. Vince turned back to his radio.

"Have sighting of the fishing boat now," the co-pilot said to the pilot.

"Right—I see it, too," said Scott. Ahead of the helicopter's flight path lay a large fishing party boat. It rocked in the long low swells of the ocean.

"Vince, give orders to that captain! Tell him to keep the same speed all the time. Tell him to turn into the wind. We must fly into the wind. That should not be hard in this weather."

"Yes, sir," said the crewman.

Scott called again to the flight mechanic. "Okay, Cal, are you about ready? Give me the position you want for the hoist."

"Yes, sir," Cal said in a firm voice. He had unfastened his seat straps. Then he hooked his safety harness to the overhead fitting. With that safety harness, crewmen could move around with no danger of falling out. Cal slid open the side door by his seat.

The white helicopter gleamed in the bright sunshine. The orange stripe near the tail marked it as a Coast Guard craft. On the front, the black nose of the radar seemed to lead the way.

The helicopter was right over the fishing boat now. The flight mechanic began to give orders to the pilot. Scott could not see the rescue litter being lowered to the boat, which rocked slowly under the helicopter. He had to listen for Cal's orders so he could keep the helicopter in the right place.

"Right, twenty feet!" Cal spoke into his helmet mike over the chatter of the rotor blades.

"Right, twenty feet," said Scott. He followed Cal's orders.

"Left, ten!" the flight mechanic called again.

"That stupid captain is not keeping his boat steady," growled Wade. "In this weather he should be like a rock under us!"

Scott did not answer. His left hand was steady on the collective. That lever worked the up and down movements of the helicopter. His right hand was on the cyclic. That lever took care of the left, right, and forward movements. His feet on the pedals worked the tail rotor. Strength showed in every muscle of Scott's body. He turned his head far to the right. He

strained to see the litter being lowered.

"Steady, steady," came the drone of Cal's voice. "Litter down on the deck!"

Now the seven-foot wire-mesh litter was resting safely on the deck of the fishing boat. The flight mechanic let extra line down. The litter must not be yanked up suddenly by a line that was too tight.

"Get off, get off!" Cal suddenly yelled. He began waving his arms at the people standing on the deck of the boat. The people looked up at Cal. He pointed to the line hanging from the chopper. Then he pointed to the coils lying on the deck. People suddenly jumped off the coils of line they had been standing on. Cal began to mutter to himself.

"Everything okay, Cal?" Scott asked.

"Okay. But we have a bunch of people who don't know what they are doing. They were standing all over the line. Wait—now they are putting the man into the litter. Steady, now. Steady. I'm starting the hoist—steady. Hold it! They're crazy!" Cal suddenly yelled. "They've dumped him over the side! He's face down in the water!"

The people on the boat had not waited for the hoist line from the helicopter to become tight. They lifted the litter to the side of the boat. Then they let it go. There was too much extra line and the litter had dropped into the sea. The victim was strapped into the litter. And he was floating face down!

"I'm going down!" the flight mechanic called. "I'm going to jump! No, wait, two men from the boat are in the water now. They are turning the litter over. It's floating safely! The man seems all right!"

"Keep steady—keep steady," Cal called to the pilot.

"Beginning hoist again—steady!"

The litter swung slowly up to the helicopter. It bumped gently against the side door. Cal pulled the litter inside. Then he closed the sliding door.

"All set," he said in a tight voice to the pilot. He turned quickly to care for the man in the litter. The man's head was wrapped in blood-soaked towels. Ocean water drained from his clothes. The flight mechanic covered the man with blankets.

Vince's report went out on the radio. "This is Coast Guard HH3F 1027 to Portsmouth Rescue Center. Rescue aboard fishing boat, *Sea Witch,* has been finished. 1027 now on its way back to Elizabeth City Air Station. Ask ambulance standby to take man to Albemarle General Hospital."

"Okay, 1027. Ambulance will be on standby," came the reply.

The tight feeling in the helicopter toned down. Each crewman carried out his own work. Cal was kneeling beside the man in the litter. Vince stayed on the radio.

The co-pilot glanced at Scott. "A really neat rescue! About as smooth as the usual bull in a china shop. You got us a real sharp flight mechanic this time. Ha!"

Scott held back his anger. Only the look in his eyes showed his feelings.

"That was not the fault of the flight mechanic. The people down below have to do their part. They should have known not to let that litter go until the line was tight and the hoist was pulling up the litter. Cal did his job!"

There was silence then, until the helicopter was over the river beside the Coast Guard Station.

Scott broke the silence. "Starting the before-landing checklist."

The crew began checking the list. The shining white helicopter hovered over the landing by the hangar. The sound of the clattering rotors shook the air. Then the craft set down gently. As the blades slowed to a stop, an ambulance rolled up beside the chopper. Cal slid the door open.

"Better luck next time," Wade called to the flight mechanic. "Hope I'll be on leave."

The flight mechanic kept to his work. He did not say a word. But his shoulders and neck were stiff under the orange flight suit.

3
Rooftop Rescue

Wade was not around for the next rescue. He was nowhere to be found.

The telephone by Scott's bed jarred him from a heavy sleep. He opened only one eye to stare at the clock. Three o'clock in the morning!

"Keane here," he said. He spoke softly. No need to wake up his wife.

"Scott, this is the duty officer at the station. Sorry to call you at this time, but you are needed. How soon can you get here?" the officer asked.

"Give me five minutes to dress. Then twenty minutes to drive out to the station. What's up?" Scott asked.

"We have a call to help at Savannah. That hurricane came ashore last night right into the city. They have three helicopters working. They need more! Our alert crew is already out on a call. We are calling your crew now. Hurry!" The officer hung up.

Scott grabbed the orange flight suit. He picked up the black boots. He could put those on in the car. His wife would know where he had gone. She was used to calls for help in the middle of the night.

It did not take Scott twenty minutes to reach the station. No policeman would have given him a ticket for speeding this time. Dark clouds sped across the sky. The area was having some bad weather, too. But at least it was not the slamming punches of a hurricane.

Scott quickly parked his car by the hangar. Only one helicopter was left on the field. A ground crew was adding fuel. That aircraft had to be the one for Scott's crew.

He went inside the hangar offices. The wind caught the door and slammed it hard.

The duty officer looked up from the map table.

"Good! No time to waste. The lowlands all around Savannah are flooded. There are reports of people drowning in their own homes. These will be rooftop rescues, Scott."

"Okay. Have you reached my crew yet?" he asked.

"Both Cal and Vince were sleeping over at the enlisted men's quarters. I can't get Wade. This was your crew's night off. He did not have to stay around. But anyway, he is not at his apartment. I checked the officers quarters, too. No one has seen him since you went off duty yesterday. I got Smith from Commander Dale's crew to co-pilot."

"Good—he's okay," Scott said. "Let's see—Vince on the radio. Cal will be on rescue and mechanics. Smith —me—we're all set."

"Right! Savannah will tell you what to do when you get closer to the city. But I have some food for you. I hope the small packages will do. There was no time to really fix you up."

"We'll do fine with what you have," Scott said. He

picked up a sack of sandwiches and hot coffee.

"Take it easy, Scott!" called the officer. Scott was already running out of the office.

"Sure . . . ," he called back.

Takeoff was slower than he wanted. The wind made the helicopter shudder. When they were in the air, there was very little talk. The only light in the black night was the glow from the panel of dials. Scott used the Loran to guide him. This told what way and how far from the base station the helicopter was. He would pick up orders from Savannah when they were near enough.

He was grateful for the way this HH3F could work. With the two engines it could search longer. It could carry more fuel. It could carry out a flight or search of more than three hundred miles.

They flew on through the dark night. Hours seemed to pass.

"Better have some coffee and sandwiches back there," Scott called to Vince and Cal. "We'll be hitting rough weather very soon. The worst of the storm has passed Savannah now. But we will feel a lot of wind and rain. And we must be ready for rescue orders. Hand us sandwiches and some of that coffee, will you, Cal?"

"Yes, sir," came the answer. Cal passed food and drink to the pilots. He handed some to Vince. The radioman was hunched over the radio. He was keeping a close check on everything.

Vince suddenly said to the pilot, "I have Savannah on the radio, sir!"

"Right!" Scott said. "Tell them how far away we are."

Heavy winds began to beat against the helicopter. Rain was blowing in great sheets on the windows. The world inside the aircraft had seemed warm and safe.

That feeling was gone now. The wind acted like a cat playing with a mouse. Any minute it could smash the chopper to the ground with one blow of its paw. The wind must have been up to sixty or seventy knots.

"Coast Guard, this is HH3F 1530 out of Elizabeth City Station, Fifth District. Do you read me?" Vince spoke on the radio.

There was a lot of noise. Then came the sound of a very tired voice. The man on duty in Savannah had been taking care of calls for help all night. He quickly gave orders to the crew of HH3F 1530.

"Twelve men still on a boat off the coast. One Coast Guard helicopter already working that rescue. Give aid as needed."

Following the man's orders, Scott quickly turned the helicopter. He flipped on the floodlights. They flew over the dark waters. It was hard to tell where land had been. Black water spread over everything. Treetops reached just above the water. They were the only flying aids to be seen. Gone were any of the usual signs for guiding the pilot. With the lights Scott could pick out the lines of trees.

"This makes me think of something I didn't like too well," the pilot spoke to his crew.

"What's that, sir?" Cal asked.

"My last station before Elizabeth City. I was flying the helicopter aboard a Coast Guard icebreaker. We were going along with a tanker bound for the Alaskan oil fields. My job was to search for a way through the ice pack. Then I would return to the ship. I'm glad they make those stations a short duty. Trying to find a path here makes me think of looking for a way through the ice!"

A blast of wind tore at the helicopter. The aircraft suddenly dropped down. Scott used all his training to handle the HH3F. He quickly touched the emergency throttle. The helicopter shook. Still Scott kept control. The HH3F answered. Its power came back strong.

"We ought to be able to pick up that Coast Guard helicopter. Vince, get him on the Tacan to show distance. The A/A position will let us speak air-to-air. He'll tell us what help he needs," Scott said to Vince.

Cal was looking out the window of the door. Rain streaked across the glass. The glare of the floodlights shone down on the dark waters under the aircraft.

"Sir!" he suddenly yelled. "Down there! There is someone on a raft or something. Circle, sir! Can you circle?"

Scott put the helicopter into a circle at once. He skimmed lower over the water. They came back to the same spot. Then they saw a person waving his arm. Rain beat down on him. They could see he was holding on to something.

Cal called out again. "Sir, that is a chimney he is holding on to! That is not a raft he is standing on! It's a house. It's almost under water!"

"Right," Scott answered. "This will be rescue number one. We can't leave a person here and go on to that boat. This one has to be first. No house can stand that strong flood of water. It might be swept away anytime! Get ready, Cal!"

"Yes, sir!" Cal was already leaping for the basket in the back of the chopper. In no time he had hooked the basket to the hoist. He slid the door open. Wind and rain tore inside the aircraft. Cal shouted to the pilot.

"Lowering basket, sir!"

The wind snatched at the wire basket. It swung wildly in the wind.

"Can't do it—can't do it, sir! The basket could slam against the person on the roof. I'm hoisting it back up. I'll use the sling. If he can hold on to that chimney, he can hold on to the sling!"

Cal quickly changed the basket. The sling was not as heavy. It would not swing with as much force.

The person down below held to the chimney with one arm. He reached for the sling with the other.

Scott twisted his head far to the right. He tried to see the sling or the person down below. If he could just see something! It was hard to fly blind.

"Good shot, sir—he's grabbed it!" Cal yelled.

Scott thought to himself, Just dumb luck! I sure can't stay steady in this wind!

"Hoisting now—here he comes!" Cal called again. Scott kept the helicopter as steady as he could.

There was a thump behind the pilot's seat. Cal had dragged in a sodden boy clinging to the sling.

"Mm-m-m," the boy tried to talk. Scott could hear the fright in his voice.

"What? What is it?" Cal asked the boy.

"Ss-s-my sister! She—she's still down there." The boy pointed to the dark waters below.

"What is it?" Scott asked the flight mechanic.

"Sir! He says his sister's down there! I don't see anybody!" Cal called above the chattering rotors.

"She's in the attic!" the boy cried. "We had to climb up to the attic. The water came up so fast. It reached the kitchen ceiling. We got on the table and got in the attic. But the water was coming up in the attic! We were trapped. I hit through the roof with an old board.

I crawled up. Then you came! But my sister! Where is she?" the boy screamed.

"I'm going down!" Cal quickly said to the pilot. "Vince can work the hoist. Maybe the girl is still alive!"

Cal put his arms through the sling. It fitted around his body. He folded his arms across his chest. This locked him into the sling.

Vince called to the pilot, "I'm lowering the hoist, sir! He's going down. Steady!"

Wind tore at the helicopter. The sling swung wildly. Cal was like a yo-yo on the end of a string. Scott kept the craft as steady as he could.

"He's okay—okay! He's on the roof!" Vince called out. Scott could hear the shaking sobs of the boy. He was slumped on the floor behind the pilot.

"Sir! He's got her! He's pulling her out of the hole in the roof. Keep it steady—steady! He's in the sling with her. I'm hoisting now. Here they come!" Vince yelled out. Scott was working his feet on the pedals. His hands were firm on the cyclic and the collective.

Then he heard the best sound. There was a thump behind him! Vince had dragged in the two wet people. Cal stood up behind the pilot. He was gasping.

"Are you okay, Nan? Are you okay?" the boy kept asking his older sister.

The young woman slumped on the floor. But she talked to her brother. "I'm okay, Jimmy. We'll be okay now. We've been saved by the flying lifeboat!"

Vince slid the door shut. The wind and rain were locked out. The chopper lifted up and whirled off to land the rescued brother and sister in a safer place.

4

Stranger on the Base

Two days later, things were back to normal at the Coast Guard Station. Scott and Wade were both on the base by 0730 hours. Vince joined them. It was muster for men coming on duty.

Cal loped in just one second before the 0755 time set for the roll call.

Wade said to Scott, "He makes me think of a camel. Same knobby knees, long skinny legs. And that dumb look on his face. I can just see him loping across the desert."

"What do you have against Cal?" Scott asked his co-pilot. Muster was over. The two pilots were standing by the coffee machine. Scott held a hot mug between both hands. He looked down at the steaming coffee.

"Wade, things aren't going well with our crew this way. Seems as if you are making sure Cal hears what you say about him. I don't like it." Scott looked steadily at Wade.

"Our brave flight mechanic should be able to take it. You think he's so great. You said more than enough about the rescues in Savannah," Wade grumbled.

"Well, things have to be settled, because something new is coming up." Scott set his coffee mug down. He folded his arms. Wade wasn't going to like the next bit of news.

"And what will be new?" Wade picked up a bag of doughnuts from his desk. He took out a fat doughnut. It was covered with a glaze of sugar.

Scott reached over to his own desk. He picked up a file.

"This is your next side duty," he said to Wade. The name on the file read Calvin A. Grimes.

The co-pilot looked at the file. "What's this?"

"You have an extra job. Part of it is helping anyone with their off-duty school. And that means Cal right now."

"What! I sure don't want to work with him. Flying with the looney goon is enough for me." Wade stuffed the last of the doughnut into his mouth.

"I hoped I would not have to do this, Wade. But I'm pulling rank on you now." Scott's voice changed. His tone was stern. "You will take care of this enlisted man's need. And the way you act toward him will have to change. Or you will find that going on your records."

"Yes, sir!" Wade said stiffly. He took the folder. "Sir, what does he need?"

Scott did not say anything for a minute. Cal had not finished high school. Scott knew what the co-pilot would think about that.

"He is trying to get his high school diploma."

"That sounds like him," Wade said. Then he caught the look on the pilot's face. "Sorry—sir—but how did he get in the Coast Guard without a high school diploma?"

"You know men can enlist without a diploma. They take certain tests. The tests show each man's skills, things he can do well. If he passes our tests, he can enter the Coast Guard. Then he can go on with his schooling while in the Coast Guard. He can finish high school or go on to college. He can do whatever he wants. That is what Cal is doing."

Wade did not say a word. He just raised one eyebrow.

The emergency siren suddenly blared. Scott and his co-pilot listened for the duty officer's voice. They tensed. They were ready to head for the helicopter.

The duty officer spoke clearly. "There is a stranger on the base. He is reported being close to the hangars. Last seen near the ready helicopter. Do not go near the stranger. He is dangerous. I repeat, he is dangerous. Our stranger is a bear. Weighs about one hundred fifty pounds, age about three years. Take care until our stranger is caught. That is all."

Scott grinned. "The duty officer had me fooled for a minute! He said a stranger was around the helicopter. I was ready to take care of that stranger!"

Wade said, "Guess the bear swam across the river from the swamp. I think I'll go out to see it. Want to come?"

Scott nodded. "For a minute, I guess. Base guards will get rid of the animal, but the ready helicopter doesn't need a bear on board."

The two pilots left their office. They began to walk rather carefully through the dark hangar. The bear could have found his way inside the big building. The wide doors were open.

"Sir, Commander Keane!" a voice yelled from just

outside the hangar. Vince ran inside the big doors. The young radioman ran up to the two pilots.

"Sir—that bear! He's just outside! I started out to look. Just as I came around the corner of the door, there he was! He stands taller than me! He doesn't weigh all that much. But he's got a mean look! Sir, where are those base guards?"

Scott laughed. "Take it easy, Vince! They'll get the bear. They had to call Animal Control in town, I guess. You don't just walk up to a bear and ask it to leave, you know. The Coast Guard could use some help on this case."

Vince stared at the officer. "Sir, I never have seen a bear. Not even in a zoo. And there he was staring at me —eye to eye. He's my size—at three years old!"

"Here, have a doughnut. It will calm you down," Wade said. He pulled another sugary doughnut from the paper bag. He held it out. And around the door came the bear! He headed right for the three crewmen.

Scott and Vince backed up quickly. They stood by the door leading into the offices. Wade was rooted to the same spot. His hand was still holding out the doughnut he had offered Vince. The brown bear did not wait to be invited. He headed right for the sugary mess in Wade's hand.

"Drop it!" Scott yelled to the co-pilot. "Drop the stupid doughnut!"

Wade dumped the doughnut onto the floor. He quickly backed away from the bear. The animal dropped down on all four paws. He sniffed at the sticky mess on the floor. His big mouth took one bite. The doughnut was gone.

"Geez, you can smell him way over here," Vince whispered to Scott. "Doesn't he smell something awful?"

"That is just a normal bear smell. They don't exactly believe in the Saturday-night bath, Vince. And he swam the river over from the swamp. That in itself is no perfume factory."

The bear was still on all four paws. A low grumble came from his chest. He looked all around him. Another low grumble.

Wade had backed up against the outside hangar door. The bear was between him and the office door. A small group of men had gathered on the edge of the blacktop outside. They were all peering into the hangar. One of the men yelled to Wade, "Here come the base guards! Your rescue is at hand!" The crowd laughed. The bear gave a louder growl. The laughing stopped.

The shaggy bear began sniffing the air. He moved his head back and forth, back and forth. Then his nose pointed to Wade again. Another growl . . .

Scott saw what the bear was after. Wade's bag of doughnuts was like a magnet to the animal.

"Wade!" he yelled. "Drop the bag! Then get out of here! Quick!"

"Wh-what?" Wade said.

The bear started a slow prowl toward the co-pilot.

"Get away!" he yelled at the animal. The bear did not like that idea. He had one thing on his mind. The smell of sugary doughnut came from that orange-suited man. The bear headed at a lope for Wade.

The base guards roared up in a jeep. The siren slowed to a whine. That did not stop the bear. His nose had found the source of that good smell. He wanted more!

Wade saw the bear coming. He headed for the nearest safe place, away from the bear. One of the choppers was just outside the hangar. Wade looked over his shoulder. The bear was loping along twenty feet behind him!

"Drop the bag, you dummy!" someone in the crowd yelled.

Wade never heard. He was scrambling up the low step of the helicopter. He fell onto the floor. His legs dangled outside. The bear reached the aircraft. He reared up on his hind legs.

There was a low whirring sound, whirring over and over. A looped rope came sailing out and landed gently around the bear. Cal Grimes stood just outside the hangar. He had lassoed the bear.

"Throw the bag to him. It will be a lot easier to make him leave," Cal called to Wade.

"Wh—the bag? Oh, the bag!" Wade looked down at the bakery sack still in his hand. The crowd began to laugh. Scott and Vince had to join in.

Wade's face flushed red. He angrily threw the bag down on the ground. The bear tore it open with one swipe. The animal stuffed the last two doughnuts in his mouth.

"Stay where you are—sir," Cal yelled to the co-pilot. "If your hands smell like those doughnuts, he'll be after them next."

Wade backed farther inside the helicopter.

The bear finished his snack. He looked around for more. But the paper sack held the strongest doughnut smell.

Scott stepped up behind Cal. The flight mechanic was still holding the rope. The bear was nosing around the paper bag.

The pilot grinned. "I don't remember anything in your file about being a cowboy, Cal. You sure sailed out a neat lasso, though."

"No, sir, I'm no cowboy," the flight mechanic said. "I used to tag bears for the Park Service back in the mountains, you know. We'd get them this way sometimes."

"Well—uh—what do you think we ought to do now?" Scott asked.

"He's leaving. I'm going to gentle him down toward the river. He just wants to go back to his swamp home anyway. Sir, can you get a couple of men to row me across? Just so we can be sure he gets back safe? I'll keep the rope on him until he's across the river."

"One boat coming up." Scott quickly gave orders to the base guards.

Cal walked slowly toward the river. He gently tugged at the rope. The bear ambled peacefully, licking the sugar crumbs from around his mouth.

Scott walked over to the helicopter. Wade was not in the doorway. The pilot climbed up the step.

"Has that crowd gone yet?" Wade angrily asked. He was sitting on the floor in the back of the aircraft.

"What does that matter? The bear has gone," Scott answered.

"So what! I'm waiting until that crowd leaves. And as for your brave flight mechanic, you know what he can do, don't you? You know what he can do with his lasso, his bear, and his diploma!"

Scott shook his head. What a mess this was turning into!

5

Search in the Swamp

The bad feelings between Cal and Wade did not get any better. Scott knew Wade felt stupid about the bear chasing him to the helicopter. People on the base had really teased him. Having Cal rescue him had only made things worse. Wade looked silly. Cal was a hero.

But this was the Coast Guard. It was not a place to let a person's feelings rule. Duty came first. Scott knew he had to do something.

The HH3F 1027 crew was on alert the night after the bear chase. They would sleep and eat on base. Then they could quickly answer any calls for help. After supper would be a good time to settle things with Wade.

Scott found the co-pilot sprawled in a chair in the officers quarters. He was turning the television dial. Scott settled in another chair.

Wade looked at him. "Hey, you're in time. They're going to show a rerun of that football game we missed. Got to see that sixty-two-yard run for a touchdown."

"Turn it off, Wade."

"Huh?"

"I said turn it off. We are still on duty and this thing has to be settled—now." Scott leaned toward Wade. His elbows rested on his knees. He held a file in one hand. There was no smile on his face.

"What thing? Oh, yeah—that Cal Grimes. Well, I've been meaning to look at his file. I'll get to it soon," Wade said.

"We'll get to it now," Scott told the co-pilot. He opened the file. "This file has not moved an inch on your desk since I put it there. Now, I can go to Commander Doyle about this. I can even go to Captain Furr. But I would rather handle the problems of our crew myself. That is, if we can work together. So, what is it to be? Me, Commander Doyle, or Captain Furr?"

"Are you pulling rank on me? So I'm a lower rank than you are—you're a lieutenant commander. Is this a threat?" the co-pilot asked. He was angry. His face was red.

Scott was not angry. He was military through and through. A job had to be done. *Semper Paratus* was more than just words to him. This Coast Guard motto was his way of life. "Always Ready"—and Scott was just that, always ready.

"This is no threat, Wade. Here's a job. Let's get it done." He looked at Cal's file. "I've checked Cal's high school records. English is the only thing he needs to get his high school diploma. English is all he has to pass. And you know you could find him a teacher for that— easy! Cal's a flight mechanic third class. I know he can go higher without a high school diploma. He can move up by showing his own skills. But he wants that diploma. And I want him to get it—fast. He's a good man. He will go much higher in the Coast Guard. You won't be able to stop him. But are you going to help him?"

Wade grumbled. "Scott, he bugs me. I never saw anyone so clumsy. He knocks things over, bumps into doors—"

Scott broke in. "But not in the helicopter, right? He's the best flight mechanic I ever worked with. And he is never afraid. Have you seen that?"

Wade rubbed the back of his neck. "Yeah, yeah. In the air he's not so bad. But, cripes, on the ground he falls over his own feet."

"But not when we need him! In the air he is a part of that helicopter. He's smooth as a cog, right?" Scott was making Wade see Cal's good points.

"Okay!" the co-pilot thundered. "Okay, I'll see that he gets his stupid diploma!"

"Good! Now why don't you get off my back? Ease up! I want to see that football game." Scott leaned back in his chair. He propped his feet up.

Wade stared at Scott a minute. Then he reached for the television dial.

The base siren called a halt to their football game. The sound jerked the two pilots up from their chairs. They were outside the officers quarters in less than a minute.

"My car—" gasped Wade. "Faster!"

The two crewmen jumped into the blue sports car. Wade roared out of the parking lot. They headed for the hangar. Their headlights cut through the wisps of fog drifting across the road.

"Um—not such a good night," Scott said. He looked out the window. A cloud cover was spreading across the dark sky.

"Slow down! Stop!" he said to the co-pilot.

Wade was used to following orders. He stopped the car. Vince and Cal were running along the side of the road.

"Hop on the back! It's quicker! No room inside!" Scott called.

Vince and Cal scrambled up on the luggage rack on the rear of the car. They grabbed the bars.

Wade drove quickly to the hangar. The ground crew was already wheeling out the HH3F. Cal and Vince raced for the chopper. Scott and Wade ran for the office.

The duty officer was talking on the hotline from the Portsmouth Rescue Center. "Yes . . . Okay . . . Yes. Got you." He hung up and wrote something on paper.

Scott looked up at the wall. He checked the machine showing wind from the northeast at fifteen knots.

"Okay—okay." The duty officer turned to the planning table. A big map almost covered the table. The three men leaned over the map.

"Right about here!" The duty officer jabbed his finger at one spot. The area was marked Dismal Swamp. "Bad place! A private plane is down somewhere in there. The last time Norfolk Airport heard from the pilot he was just about here."

Scott began making his own notes on paper.

The duty officer said, "You can't land to search. There are too many trees. I don't know what you'll find."

"Well," the pilot said, "we can give light for a search party. Who is going to be searching on the ground?"

"They have already called the county sheriff. He'll have cars out where they can drive. Then he'll use boats for the water area. That swamp is big. Boats would have

a rough time searching such an area. If you can locate
the downed plane, the men on the ground can get help
there much faster." The duty officer looked up from the
table.

"Okay, let's go, Wade," Scott said.

They were in the aircraft in minutes. Cal and Vince
were already strapped into the high-backed seats just
behind the pilots'.

Wade began the lift-off countdown with Scott. From
co-pilot to pilot went the words of the checklist.

"Throttles."

"Check," Scott said.

"RPM," Wade continued.

"Check."

"Caution panel," Wade spoke.

"Clear," Scott answered.

"Takeoff list completed," Wade finished.

Scott called to the tower on the radio, "HH3F 1027
ready for takeoff."

"Roger, HH3F 1027," the reply came. "You are
cleared to takeoff."

Scott turned the helicopter out toward the runway.

After the takeoff, Scott and Wade began to work out
their flight. They marked where they were on the chart
set up between their two seats. Then Wade worked out
the range and distance to the spot where the Norfolk
Airport last heard from the private plane.

"We have clouds at three hundred feet, Scott," Wade
said.

"Okay," the pilot answered. "Let's make passes in a
pattern at two hundred feet. We can't go any lower
over the trees in the swamp. But we should be able to
spot something."

"It will show us fire! That's for sure," Wade said.

"Don't let it be fire. We can't land to help anyone. We can only hover and give light to that area."

"Well, be sure you keep both engines going. This thing can't hover on just one engine."

Scott did not answer. Wade was not trying to teach him something he already knew. Of course helicopters don't hover on one engine.

They left behind the last glimmer of light from the smallest town. They passed across the dark land crouched below them. The swamp held its dangers close in the silent night. The helicopter's chatter rocketed into the silence.

The pilot had flipped on every floodlight that would help them to see. They made passes across the area set up for the search.

But the chopper's lights did not pick up the plane wreck. Instead the flames from the downed aircraft showed the spot.

Cal spotted the flames from the window in the side door. "There it is!" he called out.

Scott sighted the wreck from his side window, too.

Vince began reporting to the Portsmouth Rescue Center. The site of the wreck would be patched on to the men searching on the ground.

Scott circled the flaming wreck. The helicopter was flying at two hundred feet. The cloud cover stayed over them at three hundred feet.

Nothing could be seen moving on the ground near the downed plane. The helicopter flew in a tight circle. Its lights flooded the area. The small private plane had crashed beside a narrow road that curved into the swamp.

"At least the ground rescuers can get in fast by road. Look, here they come now," Wade said. He pointed to headlights bouncing over the dirt road. Not too far behind came the lights of a larger vehicle.

"Could be an ambulance. It has bigger lights," Vince said.

The helicopter moved to a good place to hover. Its floodlights were aimed at the wreck on the ground. The Coast Guard crewmen could see the men below, circling the wreck.

"They found somebody! Look over near that big tree —away from the wreck," Cal said. The floodlights picked out the men standing by someone lying near the tree. A stretcher was quickly brought from the waiting ambulance. The person was carefully carried back to the rescue car. The ambulance left the area quickly. Its red light was already flashing.

The chopper hovered for thirty minutes more. The men on the ground finally signaled with the jeep's headlights.

"It's over. They don't need us anymore." Scott put the cyclic to a forward movement. The helicopter roared off over the treetops of Dismal Swamp.

"Do you ever get scared flying this thing?" Wade asked Scott.

"Never! It's those jet pilots I admire. Get me up that high and my stomach lets me know it."

"I feel the same way," Wade said. "I even get airsick up that high! But some jet pilots tell me they can't take this kind of hovering and low flying. So maybe we aren't so bad."

"Well, you know what they say about us—we fly when nobody else will."

"Yeah—you're right. We fly anytime, anyplace."

For the first time in a week a kind of peace settled over the crew. They headed back to the Coast Guard Station.

6

What's Up?
What's Down?

The talk about jet pilots and helicopter pilots started again the next day. Scott and his crew were out on a search. A fishing boat had called in a flare sighting ten miles off the coast. Sometimes these sightings turned out to be nothing. But there was always the chance someone had sent up a flare. Each sighting was checked out.

The helicopter was flying a search pattern over the ocean. The gray-green waters of the Atlantic spread out under the low-flying aircraft. Bright sunshine shone on the sign of the crossed anchors on the orange stripe of the plane. The September day was so warm that the pilots slid open the side windows.

Vince said, "I like this kind of search and rescue. It's a vacation!"

"Don't get too lazy back there," Scott said to his radioman. "You keep tuned in to the radio. If there is a boat in trouble, maybe you'll pick up something. Cal, have you spotted anything? Any wreck—rafts—floating wood?"

"No, sir," came the flight mechanic's short answer. On board the aircraft, Cal did not join in the easy talk of the crew. He was always on the lookout for trouble. He made twice the needed checks for oil leaks or other dangers. The chopper ran smoothly. Cal made sure it stayed that way.

The HH3F chattered along the coast. One leg of the search pattern brought them close to shore. The crew could see sea oats growing on the low sand dunes. In the distance was the high, peaked sand hill called Jockey's Ridge. Then the search pattern headed the aircraft back out over the Atlantic.

Wade started the talk of jet pilots and helicopter pilots again. "So, what do you think? The high-flying boys are not like us heroes shaking our bones to pieces in this whirling bird. Why not?" he asked Scott.

Scott grinned. "Well, you know what they say the jet pilot is like. He's always blond. He is always clear-sighted with sky-blue eyes. He likes being the pilot of that bolt of lightning! Makes me wonder why you switched to helicopters, Wade. Don't you think jets are more your style?" Scott teased the co-pilot.

Wade did not catch on. "No, I'm what is known as the normal helicopter pilot."

"And what's that?" Scott asked.

"Why, helicopter pilots have deep feelings. We don't joke a lot, and—well, we like to stay to ourselves," Wade said with great pride.

"And that's why we pilot these chattering flying boats? I thought it was because we like being closer to the ground. At least, the more I fly one, that's how I feel. Seems like I like the ground better all the time." Scott chuckled. "Or maybe we just enjoy the feeling that nothing is happening right now, but any minute something will be happening!"

"Sir! I have a Mayday on the radio," Vince reported.

"See, what did I tell you?" Scott asked. "One minute passed and something is happening! Okay, Vince, what do you have?"

"Sounds crazy, sir! Some guy is screaming his head off for help! Says he doesn't know whether he is up or down."

"What channel are you listening to, Vince? Is it private or military?" the pilot asked his radioman.

"It's private, sir. I'm hearing him on 121.5—the VHF emergency channel."

"Okay, I'll take it. You keep a fix on him, Vince," Scott said.

"Yes, sir," the radioman replied.

Scott picked up the screeching sounds coming over the radio.

"Help me! Help me! I'm lost!" a man's voice yelled.

Scott spoke calmly over his radio. "This is U.S. Coast Guard Helicopter 1027. I am hearing you. Please state who you are."

"Help—" The voice broke off. "The Coast Guard! The Coast Guard hears me! Where are you? I don't see you! I can't see anything but water and sky all mixed up. Coast Guard, where are you?"

"Please stay calm. We will be able to help you. I repeat—state who you are. What are you flying? Where are you headed?"

"Oh—me? What am I flying? I'm in an Apache. Apache 402. I left Myrtle Beach a while ago. I went out over the ocean, but I got mixed up somewhere. Coast Guard, where are you? Are you a boat or a plane? I'm looking all over the place! I don't see you!" the voice babbled on.

"This is a Coast Guard rescue helicopter. We are picking you up on the emergency channel. Just do what I tell you. We will vector you in to land," Scott spoke calmly.

"Vector me—vector!" The scared voice was heard again.

"We can't come after you until we know where you are. Vector means we will . . ." Scott stopped talking. He looked at his co-pilot.

Wade raised an eyebrow. He whispered, "Sounds like we got a nut out there! Every pilot knows what vector means!"

Scott turned back to his radio. "Apache 402, are you a trained pilot?"

"Yes, but this is the first time I've been up alone over the ocean! I—aren't you going to get a line on me? You said you'd vector me in." The voice was not much calmer.

Again Scott glanced at Wade. "You do know what I mean by vectoring you in?"

"Anybody knows vector means to give me the way to fly to get out of this mess! Now come on! I want to see some land. I don't like it out here!" The voice was still shaky.

Wade said quietly, "Whew! For a minute I thought we had a non-flier lost somewhere in the sky!"

Scott sat up straighter in the high-backed seat. His voice took on a more business-like tone. "Okay, Apache 402, what does your compass read?"

"It reads ninety degrees."

"All right. Now make a one-hundred-eighty-degree

turn. Make that compass needle point due west, okay?"

"I'm turning," the man said.

"Now," Scott ordered, "start giving me a long count —one, two, three . . . slowly now. We are going to keep a check on the compass needle. Then we can get a good lock on where you are."

The man obeyed the helicopter pilot. His voice came slowly in a count from one to ten.

"Good," Scott said. His eyes were on the needle. "Now, come to a heading of three hundred to close to my point."

"Okay, I'm doing it."

"Keep steady now. You should soon sight land. When you do, tell me anything else you see. Any buildings or rivers, any landmarks. Then we'll know just where you are."

"Okay. Nothing but water yet," the man said. Several minutes passed. Then the man asked shakily, "Coast Guard, are you still there?"

Scott answered, "We are right here. We have you on our radio. And we are keeping a check on the compass needle. We'll get you in to the nearest landing field."

"Okay—okay. Thanks. Hey! I see something! There's a beach and some houses."

"Anything else, Apache 402? Anything besides houses?" Scott asked.

"Wait—yeah! Over there on the right is some kind of tall, skinny building."

Wade said, "He's seeing the monument . . ."

"Right," Scott said to the co-pilot. "Okay, Apache 402. That's the Wright Brothers monument . . ."

"Oh, yeah—the early bird brothers who flew off that sand hill! Boy, this is something!" the man shouted.

"Apache 402," Scott said quickly, "turn until your compass reads south. In other words, fly south right along the coast. Do you see a big sand hill coming up on your right?"

"Wait—yeah, and there's a lot of water behind it. Looks like a sound."

"Okay, that's Jockey's Ridge and Albemarle Sound right behind it."

"This is really wild!" the man yelled. "But I don't see you—where are you?"

"We're still out over the ocean. We'll soon be coming right behind you. Keep flying along the coast," Scott ordered.

Wade groaned. "This is something. I'm going to call it the rescue case of the year!"

The helicopter chattered toward the coast. It turned and flew in a line with the shore. Just ahead and farther inland flew the red Apache 402.

"Okay, Apache 402. You can talk with Manteo Airport now. They'll give you landing instructions," Scott said.

"Are you going to stick around until I get down?" the man asked.

There was a pause. Then Scott said, "We'll be here. That's what our job is."

The Coast Guard helicopter kept a watch over the Apache. The small red airplane was soon safely on the ground at Manteo.

The Coast Guard aircraft turned back to its own base.

"I agree with you, Wade," Scott said as he relaxed his aching shoulders. "The Case of the Year!"

7

The Breakup

The wind blasted dust across the blacktopped landing field. It made a tinny whine in the hangar doors. For two days the storm had pounded the North Carolina coast.

"About one more day to go, wouldn't you guess, Scott?" the duty officer asked the pilot.

Scott was checking the aircraft duty board. He turned to answer the officer. "These are usually three-day storms. One more day should finish it off."

"Maybe you'll get lucky. You don't need search and rescue calls until this weather breaks. Hey, would you stick by the phone? I have to pick up some papers from Captain Furr's office."

"Sure, go ahead. Take your time," the pilot said.

The duty officer left the office. The wind banged the outside door after him.

Scott turned to look at the duty board again. He wanted to check his leave time for the next few days. If the weather broke, maybe he could get one last warm day at the beach before cold weather began.

The phone rang—the red phone. That was the direct line to Portsmouth Rescue Center.

"Lieutenant Commander Keane speaking." His voice was brisk.

"Commander Keane, call the Atlantic Strike Team! We have an oil tanker breaking up off the coast at Kitty Hawk. Rescue of crew aboard is first of the things to be done. Tanker captain reports two million gallons of oil spilled. That oil must be kept off the shore. Helicopter is to drop oil booms to the tanker. Coast Guard cutter will be standing by to take on rescued crew."

Those orders began twelve hours of rescue work. Scott sounded the alarm. Then he began to get ready for a quick takeoff.

The Atlantic Strike Team was trained to handle calls for help like this one. Its group of men tried to save ships and their cargoes. They would get quickly to the site by truck, with pumps and rubber tanks for the spilled oil. The helicopter would lift two of the Strike team to the tanker. These men would see how bad the damage was. They would help place the boom around the spilled oil.

Everything had to be done to keep that oil off the shore. In four hours the boom would be in place. But beaches may be slimed with oil. Oil can kill the grasses that keep the sand from blowing away. Birds cannot fly with oil-soaked wings. Fish would be killed in the spreading oil. Speed counted!

Scott ran for the helicopter. His crew was ready. They had to wait only minutes for the two Strike Team men. Each man was fastened into a seat. Takeoff was quick, and HH3F 1027 was in the air.

The helicopter was shuddering in the gusts of wind.

Yet they were still over the land! Out over the ocean, the wind would reach seventy knots. The seas would be thirty to fifty feet high. Before this one rescue was over, Scott would easily lose five pounds. For once the pilot wished for the smooth flight of a jet. The helicopter clattered on its way.

When the aircraft reached the islands of the Outer Banks, there was trouble almost at once. A crosswind made the chopper yaw. Right to left, right to left went the sickening swing.

"Gee, sir, what's wrong?" Vince muttered.

Cal braced himself against the back of his seat. Scott had no time to answer Vince. He had to keep every thought on handling the aircraft.

The gusty wind made the helicopter yaw again. Right to left, right to left! He tried to keep the needle ball right in the center.

Wade was in tune with the pilot. He was checking the fuel gauge, the caution panel, the fire-warning light. The two pilots were a team.

Scott had a 4.0 mark among other pilots. They rated him tops—in handling his aircraft and in handling his crew. He never acted as if he had to prove anything, even when he flew with another pilot. This made Wade forget his own need to prove himself. He could become a part of this chopper, just as Scott had.

They were a team and they would carry out this rescue at all costs. Scott got the yawing under control.

Gray sheets of rain slashed needles of spray against the helicopter windows. The wind blew hard from the northeast. Sudden gusts kept knocking against the aircraft.

"There she is, sir," Cal said as soon as he saw the

tanker. Those were the first words from any of the crew for the last fifteen minutes.

The long tanker was riding low in its own sea of oil. The black mass was spreading like a big ink stain over the ocean.

"She's breaking apart at her stern!" Wade said. He pointed down to the broken ship.

"Got that oil boom ready to drop, Cal?" Scott called to his flight mechanic.

"Ready, sir! I'm just sliding the door open. Give me a hand, Vince," Cal said.

The two crewmen shoved the flattened oil boom to the edge of the helicopter and then out the door. The helicopter bucked like a rodeo horse above the flat deck of the tanker. Crewmen on the ship grabbed for the boom as it hit the deck. In no time the two men from the Strike Team were lowered to the deck, too.

"Be quick now! Get ready for rescue of the crew on that stern end! It's breaking up fast," Scott yelled over the roaring wind.

Cal hooked the basket to the hoist. The helicopter moved down to the stern of the ship. About twenty-five tanker crewmen were waiting on the deck. Wide cracks in the deck kept them from getting to the safer part of the ship.

"Ready to lower, sir!" Cal yelled to the pilot.

"Where do you want us?" Scott asked.

"Keep us right where we are!" the flight mechanic said.

"I'll try!" Scott handled the cyclic and the collective. His feet worked the pedals. He did everything he could to keep the helicopter steady for rescue.

Two of the tanker's crew came riding up in the basket. They were crouched facing each other.

"Read that sign next time, sailors!" Cal said. He pointed to the words painted on each end of the basket, "Please remain seated." "You could get tossed right out, half standing like you were!"

One sailor said, "Won't be a next time for me. I'm taking a shore job!"

Cal did not answer. He had the basket out and going down to the tanker's stern again. Then one more time, and there were six wet, oil-stained sailors sitting on the floor of the aircraft.

"Enough for now!" Scott said.

Cal pulled the basket inside. He slid the door shut. The chopper rocketed away toward the Coast Guard cutter standing by.

Lowering the tanker crewmen to the deck of the cutter was no easy job in the wild storm. But the wind seemed to be losing some of its power. As soon as one group of men was safely on the cutter, the helicopter was up and off for another batch of tanker crewmen. Back and forth they flew, from tanker to cutter, hauling men up, lowering them down. Same thing over and over, taking time only to refuel at the closest Coast Guard station at Hatteras.

That was when the fight nearly broke out. And if Cal had hit Wade, Scott would have had to report him—if Wade didn't.

Scott had stopped to check plans with the Hatteras skipper. He hurried back to the helicopter parked on the pad. Cal and Wade were standing just beside the open door. Wade's arms were crossed over his chest. A scornful look flashed across his face.

The flight mechanic was speaking in a jerky voice. "I

don't have to tell you why I didn't finish high school. People like you never understand, anyway."

"And what do you mean by that?" Wade sneered. "My understanding of people is very good, very good! I understand all people—even the lazy ones . . ."

Cal raised a fist. His face was flushed red, but not from the wind blasting the pad. His anger was so strong that Scott could almost feel it.

"What's this?" Scott strode up between Cal and the co-pilot. Neither man answered. Looks passed between them like loud signs of war.

"Get aboard—now!" Scott said. He was getting angry himself. "There's no time for such stupid talk between you two. The crew on that tanker needs us—now! So move it!"

Scott was so angry by then he could hardly control himself. No member of his crew must ever cause trouble when a rescue job was going on. He would straighten this out as soon as they were back at the station. There would be no more delay. He would either settle this fuss or he would break up this crew. He'd have them sent to other helicopters.

Four hours of hard work passed before any of the crew had time to think. Back and forth they went, from broken tanker to waiting Coast Guard cutter, with wet, shivering sailors. The sky had turned as black as the oil behind the boom. There was no light from the stars or moon.

Another six long hours passed before the helicopter clattered to a landing back at the Coast Guard Station. The four crewmen crawled out of the HH3F. Scott did not even try to make it into town to his home. He hit the bed in the officers quarters, and sleep came at once.

8

Hanging
by a Rope

Four glum men met the next morning. Scott knew the crew wasn't in very good shape. Yesterday's rescue had drained them. But another call for help could come any minute. Scott did not want to go out on a search and rescue with trouble in his crew.

He said, "I had to call you together. We need to talk."

Wade looked out the window of the office. Cal stared at the floor. Vince looked at everybody and shrugged his shoulders.

"Well, if you won't talk, I will," Scott said stiffly. "There will be no one in a crew serving with me who can't get along with the others. I've said it over and over. We are here for one thing—to search, to rescue. Now, this is the last time I try to work this mess out. Either this straightens out or it will go on your reports. I will ask Captain Furr to place each of you with other crews."

"But, sir—" Vince said.

"Not you, Vince. You're here because you are a part of this crew, that's all."

"Yes, sir," the radioman said quietly.

"Now, before we get called out again, do you think we can work this mess out or do I turn those reports over to the captain?"

The base siren answered Scott. It said no in a loud, screaming whoop. Scott's words were cut short.

"Here we go, sir!" Vince sounded happy to be getting away. Scott wasn't. Nothing had been worked out, and they were off on another call for help.

Once again Vince and Cal ran for the chopper waiting on the ready line. Scott and Wade headed for the duty officer and his big map.

The duty officer looked up from the desk. He was holding the red phone.

"Wait till you hear this one!" he said to the two pilots. He spoke a few more times on the phone.

"Okay," he said as he put the phone down. "You got a call over near Norfolk. But it's inland a ways."

"Inland? What's happening there?" Scott asked.

"Two men are trapped inside a smokestack at a power plant. They've been there since yesterday."

"What happened?" Wade asked. Scott strapped on his helmet as they listened to the duty officer.

"Two men were painting inside the smokestack. Their hanging platform tipped over. They are trapped about two hundred feet down. They have been there about eight hours already. All other tries to save them have failed, so they called us."

"How high is that smokestack?" Scott asked.

"Six hundred feet, and the report says there is a sharp-pointed lightning rod on top of the stack. That may cause you some trouble if there is much wind."

"Okay, show me where the power plant is." Scott

leaned over the big map on the table. The duty officer pointed out the site of the power plant.

"At least we don't have to search—just rescue." Wade tried for a joke. Scott did not even smile.

On board the helicopter, they stiffly went through the takeoff checklist. Scott was not making things easy for the crew. Vince looked very unhappy. Cal never talked much anyway.

After a forty-five-minute flight, Scott spotted the power plant. The two-story gray building sprawled near a stream flowing toward the James River. A tall smokestack at one end was topped by a lightning rod.

"Okay, here we go. Everything ready back there?" Scott asked.

"Ready, sir," was Cal's low answer.

"Speak louder! My neck still hurts from trying to see the hoist yesterday with that tanker. I don't want to strain to hear you. I want to hear you—not the wind! Is that clear?" Scott growled.

"Yes, sir," Cal answered. Vince hunched unhappily over his radio. Wade kept his mouth closed.

The helicopter began a circle of the smokestack. Then Scott brought it to a hover right over the opening. The two engines throbbed in an even beat.

"Watch that lightning rod," Scott ordered Cal. "Keep me clear of that! Lower your hoist when you are ready."

"Yes, sir," were Cal's only words.

Cal reeled out the line. The basket swung free. The wind bumped the basket once against the rim of the smokestack. But the line stayed clear of the lightning rod. That was more luck than skill, thought Scott. He knew he was letting his anger bother him. He knew,

too, that he could not let that happen. Angry thoughts drifting away from the controls could bring danger to this whole crew. Burned into his mind were the words posted in big letters in the hangar back at the Coast Guard Station: "One man's daydream could be a whole crew's nightmare."

Two men were trapped. They could be hurt. His anger must not cause trouble with a rescue—now or anytime.

Scott tried to change the tone of his voice. He made himself speak in a more friendly tone.

"Let's don't get fresh paint on that basket, Cal. I'd hate to mess up the inside of this chopper."

Vince gave a slight laugh. Wade started to say something, then stopped. Cal kept working with the hoist.

The line went down a hundred feet. No tug was felt on the line. Cal lowered the basket another hundred feet. Still no one grabbed the line.

"Right three feet, sir," Cal ordered.

"Right three feet," Scott repeated. "What's happening down there?"

"Nothing yet, sir. I'm lowering the line another twenty-five feet. Keep steady as we are," Cal spoke into his helmet mike.

"Steady," answered Scott.

"We've got a hold," Cal called out. "Someone down there has grabbed the basket."

Cal peered down inside the stack. From the lights being used for the painting job, Cal was able to see a little. When one man had crawled into the basket, Cal began a slow hoist—very slow. He did not want to bump the basket against the walls of the smokestack. As soon as the basket cleared the top of the stack and the lightning rod, Cal began a faster hoist. He pulled the basket inside the chopper. A man wearily climbed out onto the floor of the aircraft.

Cal turned and quickly asked him, "Are you okay for now? How is the other man? Are there only two of you?"

"I'm okay. Just bone weary. We've been down there since yesterday."

"What about the others?" Cal asked.

"Just one more—my partner. He's okay, too, I guess. We just wanted to get out of there. We've been perched four hundred feet above ground since yesterday. No supper, no sleep—too scared we'd slip."

"Okay," Cal said. He spoke to Scott. "One more, Commander Keane. Basket going down again. Make it five feet right and steady."

"Five feet right and steady," Scott said.

With no trouble from wind or lightning rod, the second man was soon pulled up from the smokestack. He and his buddy slapped each other on the back. They grinned wearily. Then they slumped on the floor.

Scott whirled the helicopter away from the towering smokestack. He landed the chopper in an open parking lot near the plant. The two painters were helped out of the aircraft. They were led to a waiting ambulance for a checkup at the hospital.

The HH3F made a quick trip to the Coast Guard Station. Scott was glad it had been an easy rescue and return trip. That didn't happen too often. He was really too beat to handle much trouble at this time.

As the helicopter neared the Coast Guard Station, the two pilots ran through the landing checklist.

Wade spoke, "Landing gear, down and locked?"

Scott replied, "Landing gear, down and locked."
The co-pilot said, "Harness, all stations locked?"
The flight mechanic answered, "Harness, locked."
Then the radioman said, "Harness, locked."
Finally Scott said, "Harness, locked."
Wade wearily said, "Brakes off?"
Scott's voice sounded the same. "Brakes off."
And the HH3F settled to the ground.

9

A Straight Hit

Ships of all kinds rode at anchor in the quiet waters under HH3F 1027. The helicopter flew over the Norfolk Naval Base in the early-morning haze.

"Cal, where did that sailor say he was from?" Scott asked the flight mechanic. The young crewman was putting the litter in the back of the helicopter. They had just brought the sailor in to the Navy hospital from his ship at sea.

"Said he was from Skunk Hollow in the Blue Ridge Mountains. That's fine land up there," Cal answered.

"He *would* think so," muttered Wade.

Scott did not listen to the co-pilot's words. "We had better check on that flare sighting reported earlier," he said. "What was that site the duty officer gave us?"

Wade said, "Fifty miles off Diamond Shoals. That was reported two hours ago when we were going out for the sailor. Do you think we still need to check it out?"

"Yes, I do," the pilot replied. They plotted the helicopter's course for the place where the flare had been sighted.

"I just thought we could get back to base for a hot breakfast. The flare was a mistake anyway, I'll bet," Wade groaned.

The helicopter flew on toward Diamond Shoals. The aircraft was going along at one hundred twenty knots.

Wade reached for the last dry doughnut in the rumpled paper bag by his seat. He tipped back the front cover of his helmet. The doughnut was just touching his mouth when the windshield of the chopper shattered. Sharp pieces flew into the cockpit.

Wade gave a quick yell. His hands flew up to his face. Scott jerked around to look at the co-pilot. Blood was seeping through Wade's fingers.

"Cal, get up here! A sea gull gave us a straight hit. The windshield shattered in front of Wade!" The pilot jerked around to check the other two crewmen's safety. As he turned, the holding piece on his life vest was suddenly pulled. These vests were worn by every crewman in flight. Each vest held a flotation bag, an emergency radio, dye markers, and flares.

Scott's flotation bag did its job at the wrong time. The bag swelled up as it should do in the water.

It was more than a surprise to Scott. The bag puffed up behind him. He fought to handle the controls right, but the swollen bag pushed against him.

"Cal!" he yelled into his mike.

"Here, sir!" Cal crawled up between the pilots. Wade was groaning. The flight mechanic turned quickly to look at him. He gently pulled the co-pilot's hands away from his face. Wade's forehead, eyes, and nose were covered with blood.

"Vince!" Cal called. "Get me my bag!"

The radioman quickly handed the first-aid bag up to

Cal. The flight mechanic set to work on Wade. He gently wiped the blood away from the co-pilot's nose and mouth. Fresh blood poured down from his wounds.

"My eyes!" groaned Wade. "I can't see!"

There was silence. Cal and Vince looked at each other. Scott had not heard the words. He was fighting to control the helicopter.

"Vince!" Scott said. "Get this bag down! Do it any way you can!"

Cal quietly turned around. He stabbed the bag with the scissors from his first-aid bag. Air hissed from the shrinking bag. Scott relaxed against his seat. The helicopter steadied under his control.

"My eyes!" Wade leaned his head against the back of his seat. Wind was whipping through the broken windshield.

"I have to get him to the back, sir," Cal said to the pilot. "This wind is battering him."

"Okay," was Scott's quick reply.

"Sir," Cal spoke to Wade. "Easy now—I'm going to get you to the back. Then I can help you better."

The flight mechanic slid his arm behind Wade's back. He eased the co-pilot sideways out of his seat. Wade blindly held on to Cal's arms. Blood was pouring freely from cuts on his face.

"Now—here—I want you to lie down."

Cal gently settled Wade into a place on the floor in the back of the helicopter. He eased the helmet off. Then he began to clean the cuts. He pressed hard on the deeper wounds. The flow of blood had to be stopped.

"Do you feel any sharp pieces in your eyes?" he asked the co-pilot. Wade had not opened his eyes.

"I don't know. I—it hurts!" Wade said sharply.

"I know—just keep still. We'll be at base quick. I don't want to touch your eyes unless I have to. A doctor should handle that, okay?"

"Okay, okay," Wade groaned.

"Vince, get over here and keep pressing hard on these forehead cuts. I want to check Commander Keane. He might need something, too."

Cal stood up. He stepped up to the cockpit. Scott had not been touched by the flying broken glass. The part of the windshield in front of him was still in one piece.

"Sir, are you okay?" the flight mechanic asked.

"Yeah—I'm fine now. That bag going up like a balloon sure surprised the heck out of me! I almost lost control of this bird, I can tell you," Scott said. "It shook me—I'll tell you! But I'm okay."

Cal looked around the cockpit. Pieces of the windshield were scattered over Wade's side. Cal looked at the dials on the panel. "Everything okay with the copter, sir?" he asked.

"I'm checking. But does Wade need you back there?" the pilot said.

"Vince is with him. I'm going back. Just wanted to check everything up here with you," Cal told Scott. Suddenly Cal was thrown against the back of the pilot's seat. The chopper's nose had pitched down and yawed to the right.

Scott fought to control the helicopter.

"Sir?" Cal asked as he straightened up. The chopper began to vibrate heavily. "Sir?"

"It's the tail rotor blades—something is wrong—the helicopter's losing power in the tail rotor blades!" Scott answered.

"Are we going down?" Cal asked slowly.

"Not if I can help it!" Scott said. "We have a chance —the power is not all gone. I've got to keep this cyclic stick right even until the pitching slows down!" Sweat broke out on Scott's forehead.

"What can I do?" Cal asked.

"Find me a good place to land—quick!" the pilot ordered.

Cal looked down on nothing but water. They wouldn't float very long down there—no good place to land . . .

"Sir . . . ," he said slowly.

"I know—no place to land," Scott said. "Well, all right—we'll just add a little power—see if this bird can get us home. But we won't be able to make a slow-speed landing. We'll turn to the left all the time at slow speed. Get back there with Wade. We'll be landing at a forward speed—straight into the wind—and level, if we can make it."

Cal quickly climbed back to the co-pilot.

"What's up?" Vince hissed. "What's wrong?"

"Nothing—" Cal shook his head. He pointed at Wade.

"Cal, how could a sea gull shatter a windshield like that?" Vince tried to keep his voice calm.

"Well, he must have been a big one. He was maybe ten, twelve pounds. He might have been traveling at thirty miles an hour right toward us. We were flying at one hundred twenty knots. That made a pretty strong smash," Cal answered.

"But the co-pilot—what do you think?" whispered Vince.

Cal spoke softly. "He hasn't opened his eyes. I don't

know about that. Some pieces of the windshield might have gone in. I can't tell. They'll find out at the hospital. But head wounds always bleed so much. It could be just cuts—or it could be a lot worse. Call in for the ambulance, Vince. We'll be coming in fast."

Vince turned to his radio.

"Cal," Wade said as the flight mechanic settled down beside him. "I can't lose my eyes . . ."

Cal was silent for a minute. "Sir, that isn't going to happen."

"Okay—okay." The co-pilot was quiet again. Cal kept holding bandages firmly over the deep wounds.

The three crewmen kept quiet on the flight. Scott kept a good forward speed, and the shaking almost stopped. They had a chance to make it back to the station.

When Vince saw the Coast Guard Station by the river, he took a deep breath. The radioman said quietly, "There's home . . ."

Scott started the landing and the helicopter began to turn left. But he kept it straight, and the aircraft touched the ground flat. When the rotor blades stopped, Wade was lifted into the waiting ambulance.

Cal stood by the ambulance. He turned to Scott. "Sir, may I go with him?"

"Yes," Scott said quietly. He wiped his wet forehead. Cal climbed into the back of the ambulance. The doors shut. The lights began to turn in red flashes.

Scott and Vince turned back to look at the shattered windshield of their HH3F 1027.

"A straight hit by a sea gull!" Scott shook his head.

10

Keep Counting

White streaks of spray flew from the tops of the waves below HH3F 1027. The sun made a cozy blanket of warmth around the aircraft.

"Man, you have to admit—it's great to be alive on days like this!" Wade said. He looked down on the gray-green waves racing before the offshore wind. This was the co-pilot's first day back on the job. Eight days in the hospital had been long enough. The cuts on his face were healed. His eyes were clear. "I do like this kind of trip. Nothing to look for—just search for the sun and rescue me from hunger! Want one?"

He held a chocolate candy bar out to Scott. The paper bag on his side of the cockpit held about five more bars.

"Not right now, thanks," Scott grinned. Whatever was making this feel like such a good day was fine with him. Maybe it was the warm sunshine or the bracing smell of the ocean air. It could be the way Wade was acting. Anyway it was a good day to be flying. Scott felt like skimming the tops of the waves—but he didn't.

"Lot of boats out today," Vince said. All four crew-men watched small boats sailing out beyond the waves that broke farther offshore. "Look at that boat with the two hulls. And a piece of canvas stretched between the hulls. What's that?"

Cal answered, "That's a catamaran—twin hull."

"Yeah, he's right. That's a catamaran," Wade said.

Scott gave a sigh. Hang in there long enough, and there's hope for better things, he thought. If the peace among this crew kept up, he would have to change his reports for Captain Furr.

The helicopter hovered near a catamaran with green and white sails. The boat had tipped over. It was lying with one hull way up in the air. Four young people balanced themselves. The boat righted itself. The crew on the catamaran waved to the men in the chopper.

Scott touched the cyclic. The helicopter whirled off farther out to sea. The HH3F skimmed easily along over the water.

All of a sudden Vince said, "Sir, I've got something on the marine channel."

"Okay, what is it?" Scott asked.

"Just a minute. It's a child's voice, I think. He's asking if anyone hears him. There he is again. Sounds like he's crying," Vince said quickly.

"Okay, I'll take it." Scott switched to the FM radio. He listened for a minute. The voice did sound like a small child. Scott spoke calmly, "This is U.S. Coast Guard Helicopter 1027. Can you hear me?"

"Y-yes, sir. Can you hear me?" the voice said.

"I can hear you fine. What's the trouble?" Scott asked.

"It's my dad. He's sick. I can't sail this boat by myself. I-I'm getting scared."

"Okay, now," Scott said in an even tone. "We will get some help to you. First, can you give me a compass reading on your boat?"

There was silence. Then the young voice said softly, "No, sir. I don't know how." Silence again. Scott was thinking quickly. No telling where the boat was. Then the child said, "But I know how to shoot those guns with lights."

"Flares! Right!" Scott said. "That's good. Can you shoot off one of those? And do you have a dye marker you can put in the water?"

Cal spoke up behind the pilot's seat. "Sir, give him just one thing to do at a time. He sounds awful little."

"Right," Scott answered. "Son, shoot the flare. We'll be looking for you."

"Okay," came a very scared reply. A few minutes passed. The helicopter crew strained to look all around. No arcing flares could be seen.

"Do you see me yet?" the child's voice came over the radio.

"Well, not just yet," Scott said. "How about the dye marker? Can you drop one of those in the water? Just throw it over the side of the boat."

"Okay, I'll do it!" the little boy said.

Again the four Coast Guard crewmen looked quickly all around. No trailing color could be seen.

"There!" the little boy spoke over the radio. "Now I'm going to do it!"

"He's just now throwing it over. Look again," Scott ordered.

"There he goes, sir!" Cal spoke quietly. "To the right and back of us—not too far away!"

Scott made a ninety-degree turn. They could see the streak of color trailing lazily from a sailboat.

"We see you, son! We'll be over you in a minute!" Scott said.

"Can you hurry?" the little boy asked. "I think my dad's awful sick."

"Coming over you by the time you count to one hundred," Scott told the child. "Can you do that?"

"Well, not all the way. I can only go up to thirty."

"Well, anyway—here we come," the pilot said.

The white and orange helicopter flew forward toward the sailboat. The sail was down. The boat was just bobbing along with the tide.

"Sir, I think I'll have to go down," Cal said to the pilot. "If the man is really sick, that child couldn't get him into the litter. I'll go down with the basket."

"Right," Scott agreed. "And Vince can work the hoist."

The two crewmen began to get things ready for the rescue. The helicopter slowly came over the sailboat. Scott had to hover with great care. The boat's mast was like a jabbing needle. The mast could punch a hole in the bottom of the helicopter. It could tangle with the cable that hoisted the basket. The pilot held the aircraft steady. He twisted his neck far to the right. That dancing mast was a great danger.

"He's going down. Steady!" Vince's voice came over Scott's mike. Then there was silence. A few minutes passed. "Okay, Cal has the man in the basket. I think he wants me to hurry, sir!"

Vince worked the hoist quickly. He swung the basket inside.

"Sir, the man's lips are turning blue!" the radioman said.

"Get that hoist back down to Cal—quick!" Scott ordered. He kept the helicopter as steady as he knew how. The basket swung out and down to the crewman waiting below. By twisting far to his right, Scott could just see Cal climbing into the basket. He held a small child in his lap. His arms were fastened tightly around the boy.

"Hoisting, sir," Vince reported.

There was a bump as the basket was pulled again into the aircraft.

"Out—quick!" Cal said to the child. He pushed the little boy toward Vince. Then the flight mechanic was on his knees beside the little boy's dad.

The dark-haired man was gasping for breath. He was very pale. Cal picked up the man's hands. He looked at the fingernails. They were bluish. So were his lips. Cal checked the man's ankles. They were swelling.

"Heart—I think it's his heart. Did your father tell you he had any pain?" he asked the child.

"Yes, sir." The little boy's voice trembled. "He said his chest hurt—and his arms. Is my daddy okay?"

Cal did not answer. The man had stopped breathing! At once Cal leaned over him. He put one hand under the man's neck and lifted. His other hand tilted the man's head back.

Then, holding him up under the neck, Cal pinched shut the man's nose. He leaned over and put his open mouth over the man's mouth. He blew into his mouth. He stopped. One—two—three—four—five. Then he

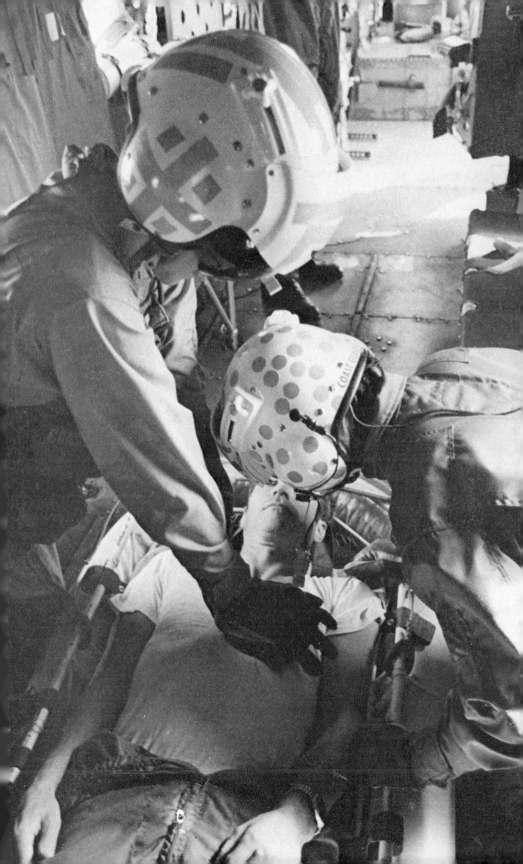

blew again—then he stopped. Wade was watching
around the back of his seat.

"His chest is rising and falling," he said to Scott.
"That's good!"

Every man on the helicopter knew what Cal was
doing. He was breathing for the man. And the rising
and falling of the man's chest meant that air was getting
through to the lungs.

Blow in—count slow five—the air came out. Blow in
—count slow five—air out again.

"What's he doing to my daddy?" The little boy stood
up. That set the crew into the next action.

"Vince!" Scott said quickly.

The radioman already knew what to do. He was on
the radio to home base at once. An ambulance would
be standing by for the man.

"Get a Coast Guard boat out here, too," Scott ordered him. "That sailboat will have to be towed in at
once. Without a crew, it is a danger to other boats and
ships."

"Yes, sir," Vince replied.

Scott wheeled the helicopter around. They must
move fast.

The little boy was still standing by his father. Cal was
counting. One—two—three—four—five—and down to
the man's mouth again.

The child started crying softly. Wade glanced away
from the control panel. He looked at the child.

"Here, sit right back of my seat. You can help us
watch these dials."

The little boy turned to Wade. He scrunched down
beside the co-pilot. Wade took a candy bar out of the
paper bag.

"Break this in two. You can have the bigger part if you can count up to thirty like you said you could," the co-pilot said.

The little boy looked up at the co-pilot in his orange flight suit. He broke the bar in half. Then he began counting slowly.

And, behind the child, Cal steadily counted five over and over. The blue color faded from the man's lips. Pink tinged his fingernails again. His chest rose and fell evenly.

Over and over again Cal breathed into the man's mouth. The helicopter flew quickly to the Coast Guard Station by the river. Scott set it down gently. The whirling blades spun to a stop.

Cal kept on. One—two—three—four—five—and down to the man's mouth. The flight mechanic kept working on the man until he was safely carried to the ambulance. The crew helped carry the man and his son inside. The man was in some pain, but he was breathing on his own.

The crewmen were standing by the helicopter. "You have any brothers or sisters, sir?" Cal asked Wade. The sun was shining on the ambulance as it raced off down the winding road.

Wade answered the flight mechanic. "I have a sister —older sister. How about you?"

"Ten," Cal said.

"Ten—ten what?" Wade asked.

"Ten brothers and sisters. I'm the oldest," Cal answered. "But I guessed you had some younger brothers or something."

"Why?" the co-pilot asked.

"You gave that kid what he needed. You gave him

something else to think about." Cal yanked his orange
sleeves down.

Wade muttered, "Oh, well—somebody had to open
that candy bar for me! I was starving."

"Yeah, I know," Cal said. He turned and bumped
into the chopper.

"Watch it there! Got to be 'always ready,' you know."
Wade touched his hand to his helmet. It was a quick
salute to Cal. Wade turned and walked into the hangar.

11

With Flying Colors

A week passed before the crew of HH3F 1027 was together again. Seven days' leave had really felt good for all of them. This first chilly day of October hinted of coming winter cold. Scott parked his car near the hangar. Muster call was too early for the autumn sun to warm things up. He reached in the car for his flight jacket.

"Hi, Scott, how did it go with you? Did you get away for a few days?" Wade stood in the open office door.

"It was good—really good. How about you?" the pilot asked.

"Let me tell you, it was great! And I have a little something going on for us later," Wade said. "As soon as muster is over, I have something set up in Commander Doyle's office."

"What have you been up to?" Scott asked.

"We better get to muster. It's nearly 0730 hours," Wade said.

"Right, don't want to be late the first day back. Have you seen Cal and Vince?"

"Oh, yeah. They're here," the co-pilot answered.

Scott spoke to his flight mechanic and radioman at muster. When it was over, he started toward the ready helicopter to check on it.

"Hey, Scott! Not that way!" Wade called. "In here— in Commander Doyle's office."

"Oh, sorry, I forgot. You've got something going on. Coming," Scott said as he turned back toward the office.

Wade, Cal, and Vince were all waiting just inside the hangar. Scott stopped when he saw the three of them standing together.

"H'm, you all look as if you know what's going on. Am I the only one in the dark?" Scott asked.

"Are you going to be surprised!" Vince said. "Man, this will blow your mind. See—"

"Vince, keep your mouth shut," Wade ordered. He glared at the radioman.

Cal thrust his hands into the pockets of his orange flight suit. He jammed his fists deep. He didn't look at the pilot. He didn't say anything. Scott couldn't guess what Cal was thinking.

"This way," Wade said. He opened the door to the offices.

"I believe I know the way to the commander's office, Wade," Scott said with a slight grin.

The four crewmen walked down the lighted hall. Wade led the way. Scott turned toward Commander Doyle's office. He caught sight of a table with a white cover . . .

And the shrill noise of the siren rose over the hangar —over the landing field—over the banks of the river. Men stopped to hear the voice of the duty officer. Everyone was listening—everyone except Wade.

He slammed his fist against the wall. "No, no, no! Not now! This will ruin it. But I'll be blanked if I'll give it up!"

He ran for the commander's office. Scott gave his co-pilot a puzzled look. Then he hurried to the office center. Cal and Vince took off at a trot for the chopper.

Scott got his orders from the duty officer. They plotted the site of the call for help. Wade still had not shown up. Scott fastened on his white helmet and ran to the helicopter.

The flight mechanic and radioman were ready. They were fastened in their seats. Wade was not in the cockpit. Scott climbed in and fastened his harness. There was a loud scrambling noise behind him. Wade came puffing up the low step. He was lugging a big brown box.

"Here, set that back there," he ordered Cal. "And keep your grubby fingers out of my box, both of you."

Scott groaned inside. More fussing again! The same old mess between the co-pilot and the flight mechanic! Then Scott got busy with the takeoff checklist. Everything else left his mind. It felt good to be back on the job. The helicopter lifted off on its first search and rescue of the day.

"What do we have this time?" Wade asked.

"If you had been with the duty officer as you should, you would know. Anyway, there is a fishing boat swamping. The motor's out. Somewhere beyond Kill Devil Hills. The call came from that area."

The early-morning sun glinted against the white helicopter. They flew quickly on their search and rescue job. Finding the fisherman was easy. Handling him was not.

They sighted the boat, straight out from Kill Devil Hills, about five miles off the coast. The motorboat was riding very low in the water. Waves were sloshing over the stern of the boat. One man was aboard. He was standing knee-deep in a catch of fish. He waved at the Coast Guard aircraft.

The helicopter made a circle. Then it hovered near the motorboat.

The man in the boat had no radio on board. He just kept waving.

"Cal, can you show him a card? See if you can find out what he needs," Scott said.

Cal printed the question in tall letters on a big piece of heavy cardboard. The man nodded his head. Then he pointed to the chopper, to a coil of rope he was holding, and then to the bow of his boat.

"Sir," Cal spoke to the pilot. "I think he wants us to tow him in!"

"What? We can't do that! We'll take him aboard and leave his boat for the shore patrol to tow in. Or he can dump his fish, and we'll drop a pump to bail his boat. Those fish are causing his boat to swamp. He's way too low in the water. No wonder his motor conked out on him."

Cal printed on the cardboard again. "Dump fish! Want pump? Come aboard chopper?"

The man shook his head hard. It looked as if he was not going to dump even one of those fish.

"Sir, he won't let those fish go! But he's going to lose his motor and his boat if he doesn't hurry and do something," Cal said.

The helicopter hovered a few minutes longer. The

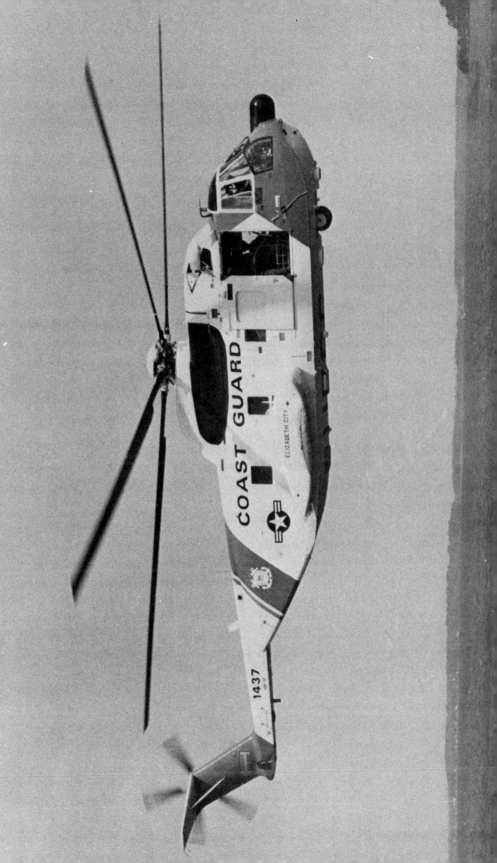

man just stood in the middle of his fish. Some still
flopped around his legs.

"Okay, Cal," Scott said. "Tell him we'll send a Coast
Guard boat out. Vince, get on the radio and ask for help
here. This one is not for us. We'll let the shore patrol
order him out of the area anyway they want to. He's a
danger to himself and to other boats, just sitting offshore like this. But who knows—maybe we would act
like that, too, if we had a catch of fish as beautiful as
that."

Cal wrote the words to the man below. The man
nodded and sat down in the middle of his fish. The
helicopter chattered off.

"Well," Wade said, "I can't wait any longer!"

He turned back to the crewmen. "Hand me that box.
We may not have a calm minute all day. I'll do it here."

Cal and Vince dragged the heavy brown box where
Wade could reach it. They squatted nearby. With the
helicopter steady on its return flight, Scott could pay
some attention to the co-pilot.

Wade seemed very proud of himself. "Well, I've
done it!" He beamed.

"Done what?" Scott almost laughed at the co-pilot.

"I've got Cal's diploma for him!" The co-pilot pulled
a white envelope out of the box. He handed it to the
flight mechanic with a sweep of his hand. "I did it!"

"You took the final test? You got the diploma? What
in heck do you mean?" Scott asked.

"No, of course I didn't take the test. Cal took it. I
coached him, so of course he passed with flying colors!
He didn't need too much, and, after all, English is one
of my best subjects—among several others, of course.

But he is not dumb, you know, and with my teaching
. . ." Wade's voice trailed off at the look on Scott's face.
The pilot was almost choking with laughter.

"What is wrong?" Wade asked.

Scott tried to stop laughing. "Nothing! I'm just laughing because—uh, well, it's just great. Uh, glad you got
the diploma for Cal. Has he been working you pretty
hard, Cal?"

"Some nights—yes, sir," Cal said quietly.

"Shoot, you should've seen all the studying Cal did on
his own—" Vince started to tell all.

"Oh," Wade said quickly. "I had planned a little
party—just some light food for us." From the brown
box he began to pull out bakery bags full of jelly doughnuts, cinnamon twirls, chocolate chip cookies, sticky
cupcakes.

Scott always tried to be ready for anything. Sometimes it was harder than other times! Helicopter training had not taught him how to handle times like this!

Scott piloted the gleaming white helicopter on its
way. He felt like a part of this aircraft. He wouldn't
trade and be a jet jockey for anything. This bumblebee
of a plane suited him fine. It could do anything. It could
stop right in midair. A jet couldn't do that! A helicopter
had stuff going around all over. It was always busy!
Something was always about to happen!

"Sir, I have a Mayday on the military aircraft radio,"
Vince reported.

"Right—we're ready," Scott said. He switched to the
military channel. "This is Coast Guard Rescue Helicopter 1027. Who are you?"

A strong voice came back. "Coast Guard, this is Navy

9404. I am losing fuel. I may have to set down before I can get back to my carrier. Can you give help if we have to ditch?"

"We're on our way," Scott answered. The white Coast Guard helicopter wheeled back out over the sea. The sun glinted on the crossed anchors.

About
the Author

RUTH HALLMAN has taught school, written books, and spent time helping boys and girls in schools, hospitals, and prisons. She lives with her husband and their four children in Manassas, Virginia. She is also author of *Secrets of a Silent Stranger,* a mystery about a man who will not speak; *I Gotta Be Free,* adventures of a teen runaway; *Gimme Something, Mister!* a Mardi Gras crime mystery; and *Midnight Wheels,* tale of a woman auto mechanic in danger.